The Recipe for Walking in
Wholeness

The Recipe for Walking in

Wholeness

JANICE HOLMES-REYNOLDS

TATE PUBLISHING
AND ENTERPRISES, LLC

Published by Tate Publishing & Enterprises, LLC
127 E. Trade Center Terrace | Mustang, Oklahoma 73064 USA
1.888.361.9473 | www.tatepublishing.com

Tate Publishing is committed to excellence in the publishing industry. The company reflects the philosophy established by the founders, based on Psalm 68:11,
"The Lord gave the word and great was the company of those who published it."

Book design copyright © 2013 by Tate Publishing, LLC. All rights reserved.
Cover design by Jan Sunday Quilaquil
Interior design by Mary Jean Archival

Published in the United States of America

ISBN: 978-1-62510-970-5
1. Religion / Christian Life / Spiritual Growth
2. Religion / Christian Life / General
13.02.21

Contents

Introduction

G rowing up I attended church every Sunday. I was baptized with water at the age of twelve because I wanted to sing in the church choir. In order to sing in the choir you had to be a member of the church. As I grew older I started asking questions. It reminds me of being two years old all over again. I started asking questions. Why are we here on earth? What is our purpose for being here on earth? When was the beginning of the world? What is my purpose? Why are there are so many denominations? I would receive answers that would prompt more questions. Then I would wonder why some parts of the Bible were not discussed.

Something in my spirit would tell me there was more, and I wanted to know everything. I began reading my Bible and other books that talked about Jesus and what actually took place on the cross, about Faith and the Holy Spirit, The Baptism of the Holy Spirit and speaking with other tongues. I was later baptized with the Holy Ghost, which was over twenty years ago. I have been studying the Bible ever since.

While reading the Bible I began to receive revelation of the scriptures and there meanings, and was directed to other confirming scriptures. I felt peace in my Spirit. The Scripture says when we know the truth, our Spirit will bear witness. We are living in a time where people are looking for answers to questions such as: Why are my prayers not answered? Why does everything seem to be a struggle? Is there any hope for the future?

In this book I will speak on my personal experiences and journey as Jesus Christ, through the Holy Spirit revealed himself to me. How there is hope for every believer, and we can walk in health, healing, prosperity, wholeness, soundness, and deliverance, which are the true blessings of God.

Holy Spirit the Person

Starting with the basics, salvation occurs when you accept Jesus as your personal Lord and Savior.

> That if thou shalt confess with thy mouth the Lord Jesus, and shalt believe in thine heart that God hath raised him from the dead, thou shalt be saved."
>
> (Rom. 9:10)

The Holy Spirit is with you the moment you invite Christ to come into your heart and become born again or saved. The word *save*, both in the Old Testament and New Testament, means: health, healing, prosperity, to be made whole, soundness, preservation and deliverance.

However saying the prayer of confession, also known as the sinner's prayer, and being baptized with water is just the beginning. You can go further in your walk with God. Just as you were baptized into the body of Christ, now Jesus Christ wants to baptize you with the Holy Spirit and Power. Remember, Jesus did not do miracles, signs, and wonders until after He was filled with the Holy Spirit.

> I baptize you with water; but He will baptize you with the Holy Spirit.
>
> (Mark 1:8)

Being "filled" with the Spirit and speaking in other tongues is where He imparts His presence and His gifts. Receiving the Holy Spirit is an added benefit. It allows you to live in a higher level in Christ where He imparts his wisdom and understanding of spiritual things.

> But ye shall receive power, after that the Holy Ghost is come upon you (Act 1:8), and they were all filled with the Holy Ghost, and began to speak with other tongues, as the Spirit gave them utterance.
>
> (Act 2:4)

Many people think that praying in tongues is a gift for only some people and not available to all. Speaking in tongues is a gift, but it is a gift that is available to every believer much like salvation.

> In Acts it says that God is no respecter of persons.
>
> (Act 10:34)

God will not make something available to some people and not others. Praying in tongues allows the Holy Spirit through you to pray in a beautiful prayer language directly to the Father. It is not scary or spooky; that is a lie of the Devil to keep Christians from operating in the power and authority that God has made available to them. Praying in tongues is a tool that will benefit every believer in their prayer life and should be utilized often.

How awesome is it when you can pray for every situation in your life concerning family, friends, job situations, relationships, sickness, and whatever else is weighing on your heart, without having to think of the perfect words to pray because your Heavenly Father through the Holy Spirit knows exactly what you need to pray. Praying in the Spirit is like laying a track so when you get down the road you will not be derailed. Can you imagine how great it would be to pray in the Spirit and stop a disaster from taking place in your life ahead of time. I believe this is why Paul said to pray without ceasing. Praying in the Spirit provides a covering.

> Likewise the Spirit also helpeth our infirmities: for we know not what we should pray for as we ought: but the Spirit itself maketh intercession for us with groanings which cannot be uttered.

> (Romans 8:26)

> Pray without ceasing.

> (1 Thessolonians 5:1)

> Which things also we speak, not in the words which man's wisdom teacheth, but which the Holy Ghost teacheth; comparing spiritual things with spiritual.
>
> (1 Corinthians 2:13)

Think about a student who has an important exam coming up and he is praying, Lord help me to do well on the test. However, if he were to pray about the test in the Spirit, or his prayer language, the prayer may cover specific things that the boy is not aware that he is praying, because the Spirit knows exactly what needs to be prayed. Therefore, the prayer may actually cover things like "Cause me to receive an A," "Keep me from being distracted," and "Cause me to focus," "Cause me to recall all that was discussed during the lecture." His Spirit would be praying things that our intellect might not think to pray. Again, it says that we do not know what we pray, but the Spirit knows exactly what we need to pray.

God is a spirit, and who better to teach us spiritual things than the Holy Spirit? But the Comforter, the Holy Ghost, whom the Father will send in my name, he shall teach you all things, and bring all things to your remembrance, whatsoever I have said unto you (John 14:26). God invites all of humanity to live in his presence. Simply learning how to pray with your whole heart will allow you entrance into the very presence of God.

Draw nigh to God, and he will draw nigh to you.

(James 4:8)

Let us draw near (to God) with a true heart.

(Hebrew 10:21-22)

Another benefit of praying in tongues is that it will build your faith.

But ye, beloved, building up yourselves on your most holy faith, praying in the Holy Ghost.

(Jude 1:20)

If you want to begin praying in the spirit or be filled with the Holy Ghost, it is very simple. You might start by saying, "Holy Spirit, come into my heart and help me pray now."

Jesus said, if ye then, being evil, know how to give good gifts unto your children: how much more shall your heavenly Father give the Holy Spirit to them that ask him.

(Luke 11:13)

That is exactly what He wants you to do—ask Him. The Bible says, "He prays for you with groaning that cannot be uttered" (Romans 8:26). And when you begin to pray you will feel your burdens being lifted. Have you ever felt heaviness on your heart? Some people may refer to it as stress; others may describe it as a burden or uneasy feeling of worry, and sometimes you can't identify what it is. When you pray in the Spirit you began to pray through those burdens because they are being taken care of in the spiritual realm. You began to feel a release and the heaviness leaves and you feel a sense of peace.

After you ask the Holy Spirit to help you to pray open your mouth and begin speaking something, not necessarily words but sounds; the Holy Spirit needs something to work with. If you sit there with your mouth closed it will not happen. Try saying words with long syllables, like saying hallelujah several times. Don't worry about how it sounds. Keep your focus on Jesus and his goodness and knowing that it is His will for you to speak in this heavenly language. If you truly want it, it will turn into a different language. Don't over think things. Lift your hands in praise and let it flow.

When it starts flowing don't stop, but continue to practice speaking. Don't let the enemy trick you out of the blessing. Remember the last thing the enemy wants is for you to walk in the authority and power that God intended for you to walk in. He wants to keep attacking you in your home, finances, family, and health. This is a tool that you need to successfully defend yourself against those attacks. So when you receive the thoughts that it sounds silly, or you're just speaking gibberish, ignore those thoughts. You are most likely praying in tongues. Please don't give up.

Relationship with the Holy Spirit

The Holy Spirit is a person; He is the power the One who carries out the work of the Father and the Son. The Holy Spirit was sent from heaven to protect God's interest in your life. It is His desire to comfort, direct, convict, and empower you the way that Jesus would if He were here on this earth. The Holy Spirit is God also. He is equal with the Father and the Son, and He wants a personal relationship with you. He longs for fellowship with every believer and wants you to ask him questions. He will reveal the answer. Have you ever overheard someone talking about a problem and you knew the answer, but you could not tell them because you were not a part of that conversation? Well, that is how the Holy Spirit feels. We talk about a problem, crying and stressing, and saying, what am I going to do?

But we never think to ask Him, "Holy Spirit, what should I do in this situation?" He has the answer and will reveal it to you. Remember He is here on this earth to help you. He lives on the inside of every believer.

I recently heard Joel Osteen telling a funny story about a man looking for a parking space. He went around and around trying to find a parking spot.

He said, "Lord, if you will cause me to find a good parking spot I will attend church every Sunday." Immediately the man found a parking spot right up close to the store. He said, "Never mind, Lord, I found one.

Isn't that what Christians do sometimes? We ask for help and when things work out the way we want, we discount it as if it were something we did in our own strength or consider it a coincidence. The Holy Spirit speaks to us and directs us on a daily basis, but because we are so busy and never stop to quiet ourselves we sometimes miss what is being said or never give Him credit when He does provide an answer. We are busy every day at work, or attending to the children, and then finally at night you would think we would allow for quiet time for the Lord to Speak to our hearts, which is the Spirits, we leave our televisions on all night because we are use to the noise. When do we yield to hear from the Spirit?

The Spirit talks to us all day every day. How does the Holy Spirit Speak to you? By knowing in your heart, a prompting, a sense of urgency, directing you to scripture, a still small voice that you will hear in your inner man (spirit), through spontaneous thoughts. And on occasions he will speak to some with an audible voice.

> For as many as are led by the Spirit of God, they are the sons of God.
>
> (Romans 8:14)

> Howbeit when he, the Spirit of truth, is come, he will guide you into all truth.
>
> (John 16:13)

In addition, when reading the Bible He will explain the meaning of the scriptures to you and lead you to other passages confirming the word. There was a time when I would wonder how people could sit and read the Bible. Every time I would try to read it, I could not read past two chapters. What do you think I did? I asked the Holy Spirit to give me the desire to read the Bible, and now I read it all the time. The Spirit makes the pages come alive, and the reading is so very interesting. That is the reason the Bible is called the *living* word.

If you are one that has difficulty reading the Bible, try reading the Amplified Bible. When you begin reading the Bible on a regular basis, the hidden mysteries will be revealed to you through the Spirit of Revelation, and you will start to develop an understanding of the Word and the things of God, and a relationship with Jesus and the Holy Spirit begins to form. Every believer can receive revelation, and revelation is what builds your faith. It is the Spirit of revelation that opens up our knowledge of who God is.

The Holy Spirit is a gentleman and He does not invade your space unless you invite Him. He will not come into your room unless you invite Him in. He does not speak to you until you speak to Him. How long will He wait? It could be weeks, months, or even years, as long as you wait. You will never know His power or His presence unless you ask Him. "Holy Spirit, tell me about Jesus, or teach me about the things of God."

Ask, and it shall be given you; seek, and ye shall find; knock, and it shall be opened unto you.

(Matthew 7:7)

Understanding the Trinity

A major change took place in my life when I realized that the Holy Spirit is God. Many people—my self included—are somehow brought up to believe that He is less than equal. We have adopted the thinking that because He comes third, He is not really God. The Holy Spirit is God. He is just as much God as Jesus and just as much God as the Father.

We know that the Trinity is made one by three persons. However, many still have trouble with the full understanding of that. I used to think of it this way: My name is Janice, but I can be called wife, mother, or daughter, although I am still one person. However, I believe that the Trinity is three individual persons that are all connected, or closely knit together. Some of us have been in church for many years and do not have a clear understanding of the Godhead. The enemy has made people to ashamed to ask. Especially if you have attended church for many years you begin to feel condemnation, and condemnation is not from God.

There is therefore now no condemnation to them which are in Christ Jesus, who walks not after the flesh, but after the Spirit.

(Romans 8:1)

Satan wants to shame you and keep the body of Christ in darkness and ignorance.

> My people are destroyed for lack of knowledge.
>
> (Hosea 4:6)

Understanding the Godhead

First we must understand that each person of the Godhead is equally as important as the other and we are to worship, praise and thank all three.

1. God the Father—created all things. He is the Originator: For by him were all things created, that are in heaven, and that are in earth, visible and invisible, whether they be thrones, or dominions, or principalities, or powers: all things were created by him, and for him. (Colossians 1:16)

2. God the Son—Jesus, He is the Administrator: The word *administers* in the Dictionary means to be responsible for the implementation or use. Another translation is to have charge of: to give or apply. Jesus spoke God's word throughout the earth. Jesus is the Word that became flesh. And the Word was made flesh, and dwelt among us, and we beheld his glory, the glory as of the only begotten of the Father, full of grace and truth. (John 1:14) It is because of Jesus that we have access to God the Father.

3. God the Holy Spirit—The one who exhibits the Power. It is through the power of the Holy Spirit that causes the Word to manifest in this natural realm. When Jesus spoke the word and administered signs and wonders, the Holy Spirit was the power that caused the manifestation. The Holy Spirit is our comforter; He leads, guides, directs, and teaches the body of Christ, and we should seek a relationship with him to understand the mysteries of the Kingdom. Because it is given unto you to know the mysteries of the kingdom of heaven. (Matthew 13:11)

How Faith Works

Until you truly understand the fact that God is good and you can trust Him with your life, your faith is never going to be great because you will always draw back in fear. You will always be thinking, *What if He doesn't come through for me? What if He is not listening to me? What if He asks me to do something that will harm me in some way?*

> But without faith it is impossible to please him: It is vital that you understand that faith is the opposite of fear.
>
> (Hebrew 11:6)

> For God hath not given us the spirit of fear; but of power, and of love, and of a sound mind.
>
> (2 Timothy 1:7)

I had a friend that was afraid of everything; you name it and she was afraid of it. She would say that she didn't want to be buried when she died. She was afraid of bugs. Even though she was the sweetest person you would ever want to meet and she loved the Lord, she walked in fear her whole life and because of that her mind was not at peace. She did not sleep well at night because she was always worrying about something.

> It is vain for you to rise up early, to sit up late, to eat the bread of sorrows: for so he giveth his beloved sleep.
>
> (Psalm 127:2)

It is important to focus on faith rather than fear. Faith is of God, and fear is of the enemy. He wants every believer to walk in fear so he can keep the body defeated.

> Now faith is the substance of things hoped for, the evidence of things not seen.
>
> (Hebrew 11:1)

Faith is when you pray for something and you believe you have it before it can be seen in this natural realm. For example, if a person is sick and believing for their healing, they must first believe that Jesus died on the cross and bore their sickness and disease. In addition, they must believe that it is His will for them to be well. How do we know that? The Word states that all through the Bible. Then you must create a mental picture in your mind's eye seeing yourself with the desired results, even when everything around you looks the opposite.

Then we begin to focus on the Word of God. You do this by reading the Bible, reading other faith based books, listening to CDs of sound teaching, and listening to Christian music. This will build your faith.

> So then faith cometh by hearing, and hearing by the word of God.
>
> (Romans 10:17)

The Bible says that the eyes and the ears are the window of the soul. This means that whatever you are putting before your eyes and ears is in your spirit (heart). If you are putting eight hours of reality TV before your eyes, then that is what is in your spirit. If you sit on the phone and gossip, slander, murmur, and complain all day that is what is in your spirit. So when a serious event in your life arises, what do you have to draw on? Only what is in your Spirit. If you speak positive words, faith building words reciting scripture, you are building your faith. That is what is in your Spirit and that is what will rise up in you when facing a serious situation, or believing for specific answers to prayers.

My Trip to China-Testimony

I had a situation where I had to stand in faith. I felt being led to attend a mission trip in China. At that time the trip was not in my budget. My husband said that if you are meant to attend the trip, the Lord will see to it that the funds are made available for you to go. He took my hand and we said a prayer and were both in agreement.

> Again I say unto you, that if two of you shall agree on earth as touching anything that they shall ask, it shall be done for them of my Father which is in heaven.

> (Matthew 18:19)

We must understand what powerful tools the Lord has put in place for every believer to be successful here on earth. The words in the Bible are there for us to walk in victory. To continue, after we prayed it was settled in both of our minds. I was going to China. I had never been on an international trip before. I was so excited, and began telling people I was going to China. I told my family and friends. Now let me ask you, do you know when that prayer was answered when we prayed for it?

> What so ever ye desire, when ye pray, believe that ye receive them, and ye shall have them.

> (Mark 11:24)

Don't wait until the manifestation comes. I had to stay faith focused. I knew without a doubt that I was to attend that trip. It was revealed to me that after attending the trip my life would never be the same. I started thinking I had to attend. However, the extra money had not come in. The date was quickly approaching, and I had told everyone I was going.

At that point the enemy tried to instill fear in me. The thoughts of how embarrassing it will be if you don't get to go after telling everyone, frightened me. Immediately I had to speak to those thoughts, quoting scripture and saying out loud, "Devil, you're a liar. My God supplies all of my needs according to His riches in glory." When you believe for a prayer to manifest, you must quickly find scriptures that pertain to that situation and speak them often. By this time I had been telling people for months that I was going to China. Because I did not have the funds, I had not registered for the trip or applied for the China Visa. However, I was firm in my confession.

"Thank you, Lord, that I am going to China." I would sit in my backyard on my patio looking up at the airplanes; our home is located in a flight path. I would confess, "I will be on an International flight to China. Thank you Jesus." I would visualize it in my mind, sitting on the airplane and eating the meals. It was getting really close to that time and it truly looked as though I was not going on my trip. Everything in this natural realm said I would not be going to China.

I was under so much pressure the devil would come at me with thoughts such as, *Look at you now. What are you going to do? What is your mother going to think?* I even entertained the thought that maybe it's not God's will for me to go, but I knew that was a lie because the trip was to do His work. The devil really wanted me to give up on that trip.

If I had at anytime believed that I was not going or confessed words contrary to what I had prayed, I would have missed out on the trip—a true blessing. I was determined not to yield to the pressure of fear doubt, and unbelief because I would have forfeited my trip. That is how the enemy is able to steal our blessings.

However, when you are at the point of testing is the time when you are closest to a breakthrough, and it is very important how you handle the situation. Are you going to believe what you see and how things appear, or will you operate in faith and believe what the Word of God says? You have to choose. This process is the same when standing on healing or any other situation you have prayed about.

> For verily I say unto you, That whosoever shall say unto this mountain, Be thou removed, and be thou cast into the sea; and shall not doubt in his heart, but shall believe that those things which he saith shall come to pass; he shall have whatsoever he saith.
>
> (Mark 11:23)

> Therefore I say unto you, What things so ever ye desire, when ye pray, believe that ye receive them, and ye shall have them.
>
> (Mark 11:24)

God is not a man, that he should lie; neither the son of man, that he should repent: hath he said, and shall he not do it? or hath he spoken, and shall he not make it good?

(Numbers 23:19)

The Bible provides a scripture for every situation in life. And God will honor his word. It was a matter of days before the trip and the extra money came in. I was able to register for the trip, pay my airfare, and get my China Visa just in time. Praise the Lord! I don't think I ever quit smiling the whole trip; it was an awesome experience and an emotional one. I sat on that plane eating my meals just as I had envisioned a few days prior sitting in my backyard. I was flying for a total of fifteen hours and was at awe at how things turned out.

God is so real and wants us to depend on him. He was right; my life has not been the same since I have been back. My relationship with Him is on a whole different level.

That is how faith works; we have to walk it out. It may seem difficult at first, but as you get to know God's personality, you will become convinced His word is true.

Faith Confession

Father, in the name of Jesus, I am a believer and I believe Your Word. I can have what it says I can have, and I can do what it says I can do. I cause to be of no effect any and every word that I have spoken or thought that does not line up with the Word of God. From this moment on I will only think on things that are honest, just, lovely, pure, and of a good report. I am confessing it now, out of the good treasures of my heart, only good things will come to pass.

I am the righteousness of God, and I have the God kind of faith, ever increasing limitless faith. I am a new creation, an heir to the throne, and a joint-heir with Jesus. I have been delivered from the power of sin and death and redeemed by the blood of the lamb, redeemed from the curse of the Law, poverty, sickness, and death.

I can do all things through Christ who strengthens me. I am more than a conqueror. Greater is He that is in me than he that is in the world. Therefore, I can overcome every situation. I have the God kind of faith residing in me, and through faith I have the victory that overcomes the world.

Father in the name of Jesus, I thank you for giving unto us all things that pertain to life, and godliness. I believe in my heart, and speak with my mouth that those things which I confess will surely come to pass. In Jesus name, Amen!

Taking Control of Thoughts

This is an important chapter because most people do not realize that their battles are won and lost in the mind. What thoughts are you thinking on today? What worries are you focused on?

> As a command be careful for nothing; but in everything by prayer and supplication with thanksgiving let your request be made known unto God. And the peace of God, which passeth all understanding, shall keep your hearts and minds through Christ Jesus.
>
> (Phillipians 4:6-7)

The Amplified Bible says, "Do not fret or have any anxiety about anything."

> Finally, brethren, whatsoever things are true, whatsoever things are honest, whatsoever things are

just, whatsoever things are pure, whatsoever things
are lovely, whatsoever things are of good report; if
there be any virtue, and if there be any praise, think
on these things.

(Phillipians 4:8)

Do you replay in your mind past hurts and disappoint-
ments? Do your conversations include discussions of what
a person did to you many years ago? Although these things
can be traumatic, you cannot continue rehearsing the events
of what happened in your past. It will literally eat you up
inside and you will never heal from it. Satan wants you
to stay in that place of hurt, bitterness, and unforgiveness
because it opens to a door for him to cause havoc in your
life. As hard as it may seem, you must forgive. Forgiveness
benefits you.

For where envying and strife is, there is confusion
and every evil work.

(James 3:16)

If you will practice what I share with you, this will be
the last day you will ever have a worried thought. You can
commit yourself and all the cares and worries of your mind
to Him and enjoy divine peace. God is against worry. It
does not produce anything but stress, strain, and death. The
whole Bible is against worry because Satan designed it.

Humble yourselves therefore under the mighty hand of God, that he may exalt you in due time. Casting *all* your cares upon him.

(1 Peter 5:6-7)

Your confession every morning should be, "I do not have a care because I roll all of my cares over on the Lord." Now cast out every worried thought that would make its way into your thinking. For example, let's say you gave a suit away to someone that needed it. Later, another person comes and asks you about that same suit. You would say that you gave that suit away. Well, that is how you should handle your cares. We must cast them over on the Lord and not take them back.

If Satan brings a worried thought to your mind, saying, *What if God doesn't come through?* You can tell him to talk to God about it. It no longer belongs to you. Many people want God to miraculously remove their worries. But that is not how to get the peace of God. God's peace comes from acting on His word. And the Word says you must replace those thoughts with the Word. You are the one that must keep your thoughts under control.

Casting down imaginations, and every high thing that exalteth itself against the knowledge of God, and bringing into captivity every thought to the obedience of Christ.

(2 Colossians 10:5)

It can be dangerous to allow these thoughts to continue and fester because when you think on a negative thought for an extended period of time they become strongholds. A stronghold is an incorrect thinking pattern that has molded itself into our way of thinking. These strongholds have the capability to affect our feelings, how we respond to various situations in life, and they play a large role in our spiritual freedom.

When Satan gives you the thought that you will never see the manifestation of your prayers, it is time to gird yourself with the truth.

> Having done all to stand, stand therefore, having your lions girt about with truth.
>
> (Ephesians 6:13-14)

> Jesus said, "Thy word is truth." (John 17:17) Therefore, speak the truth to those thoughts, speak the Word.

Find scriptures pertaining to your current situation. Do a search on scriptures that pertain to your current situation, such as Scriptures on healing, finances, marriage, prayers for husbands, prayers for wives, and prayers for addictions or deliverance. In addition, there are concordances on the computer. There are no excuses.

Do not entertain those thoughts of doubt and unbelief. Satan has no power over a believer. We have the authority that has been given to us by Jesus dying on the cross. The only way we are defeated is when we walk in doubt, fear, and unbelief. The power of God begins to operate when you cast your cares over on Him. As long as you worry about it, you only hinder the flow of His power and tie His hands. Satan cannot steal our blessings, but he can cause you to surrender it, by giving up.

If you find yourself faced with a situation that deals with your health, and the doctor's have given you a severe diagnosis, the first thing you should do is start speaking those scriptures that pertain to healing. Speak the scriptures the same way you take medicine. Get it into your spirit; it will build your faith.

Remember Satan will come to you with thoughts of defeat. He makes suggestions like: *It won't work this time*, *What if the doctors can't heal this type of disease?* or *But you know what happened to uncle Bob!* Immediately cast those cares, and speak the word. Speak to those thoughts by saying, "The doctors may not be able to heal this type of disease, but with God, nothing is impossible," or "Maybe it didn't work for uncle Bob, but it will work for me because I am a child of the Almighty King, and His Word says, 'Beloved, I wish above all things that thou mayest prosper and be in health, even as thy soul prospereth'" (3 John 1:2).

In addition, write the scriptures on sticky notes and put them on your bathroom mirror, or on the refrigerator. Speak them regularly and tell God, "I am confessing your word; this is what you said belongs to me as a believer." Remember the Bible tells us that God's Word will not return unto Him void. That situation will turn around. Praise God!

So, what difficult situation are you facing today? Start putting these principles into practice. Find scriptures that pertain to that situation and use your mouth. If you are not facing any problems in your life right now, good; but it would be wise to start applying this principle now, to be equipped to handle any situation that may arise in the future.

God Wants You Healed

If a person has limited revelation in an area of healing and doesn't believe that healing is for today, then he will not see many healings take place.

When Jesus sent His disciples out, He instructed them to preach the Kingdom of God and to heal the sick (Luke 9:2). He placed no limitation on the sick; any sick were to be healed if they would receive it. The disciples were told to freely give what they had received. Many people today believe that healing belonged to the early church. The church today is no different than the early church with the exception of the fact that we now have an even better covenant.

> And Jesus went about all Galilee, teaching in their synagogues, and preaching the gospel of the kingdom, and healing all manner of sickness and all manner of disease among the people.
>
> (Matthew 4:23)

Jesus Christ the same yesterday, and today, and forever.

(Hebrew 13:8)

God intended for his people to walk in divine health. Under the old covenant, God promised His people immunity from disease.

And ye shall serve the Lord your God, and he shall bless thy bread, and thy water; and I will take sickness away from the midst of thee.

(Exodus 23:25)

That promise is even stronger under the new covenant. Isaiah, looking forward to what Jesus would accomplish at the cross wrote, "Surely he (Jesus) hath borne our griefs, and carried our sorrows. He was wounded for our transgressions, he was bruised for our iniquities: the chastisement of our peace was upon him; and with his stripes we are healed" (Isaiah 53: 4-5).

The Apostle Peter, wrote concerning the same event stating, "…by whose stripes ye were healed" (1 Peter 2:24).

Were healed is past tense. Meaning Jesus finished your healing on the cross. He paid the price for you to be whole—spirit, soul and body.

We all wonder why so many people are sick if it's God's desire for us to be well. Many of us are just not willing to do what it takes to be well. We are first spirits; we have a soul which is our mind, will and emotions, and we live in a body—our earth suit. We all want to be well, but to be well we have to make the right choices. I remember working with a lady that was diagnosed with breast cancer. She had lost her hair and had a really rough time, but praise the Lord she is a survivor. I was talking to her one day, and she was so happy that her hair had grown back. It was curly and beautiful.

She said, "I always wanted curly hair." A few months later I would see her on breaks smoking her cigarettes. I would say that was not a wise choice to make. We have to do our part, and take care of this earthly suit. Just as we have to feed our earthly body with healthy nutritious food, we also have to feed our spirit man. The Word is actually spirit food.

Likewise, everything in the Bible deals with sowing and reaping; it is a spiritual Law. If you sow money you reap a financial harvest. If you want health you need to plant seed that will eventually reap a healing harvest.

> My son, attend to my words; incline thine ear unto my sayings. Let them not depart from thine eyes; keep them in the midst of thine heart, for they are life to those that find it and health to all their flesh.
>
> (Prov. 4:20-22)

If you have a good reference Bible, you will notice a little number or letter by the word "health." The marginal note will indicate that in the original Hebrew, the word translated "health" was originally the word "medicine." In other words, God is saying, "My words are medicine to all their flesh."

As you feed on the Word you will become spiritually and physically strong. When you meditate on the Word it is like taking God's medicine. Do you know any medicine that will cure you after just one dose? No, nobody does. Therefore, you are not going to take just one dose of the Word and get well either. If you are faithful to take it continually, it will eventually be hard to get sick.

Remember in the last chapter we talked about thoughts and how to combat those thoughts with words. The words we speak are very important, and they have power. God made man in His likeness. In the beginning, God the Almighty Creator spoke things into existence. He has given us that same creative power through our words. What comes out of our mouth, good or bad, is what we create in our lives. "Not that which goeth into the mouth defileth a man: but that which cometh out of the mouth, this defileth a man" (Matthew 15:11).

What is coming out of your mouth? Gossip, slander?

When our children were young and would catch a cold the first thing we would ask them is if they commanded that cold to leave. I would hear them saying, "Cold, I command you to go, in Jesus name." It was so cute. There is not greater faith than that of a child.

> Train up a child in the way he should go: and when he is old, he will not depart from it.
>
> (Pr. 22:6)

There was a time when my youngest son had a speech impediment. He would stutter. He was in elementary school the first or second grade and we had a discussion about his speech. Like everything else I told him to pray and ask God to correct his speech.

A few weeks later we were in the car having a conversation and he said, "Mom, did you notice I don't stutter anymore?" It hit me like a ton of bricks because I did not realize. I had not noticed until it was bought to my attention.

I said, "How did that happen? When?"

He said, "I prayed about it like you said."

That really blessed my heart; he was so young and precious. Praise God!

Don't wait until you have a need, start to train yourself now. What is in your heart is what will come out of your mouth. If you want to see your desires come to pass, you need to make your words match your prayers. Don't pray in faith and then turn around speaking words of unbelief.

Again, healing is for today. God has always provided healing for His people through His covenant; He will heal anyone who believes. God will not only heal you, but use you to minister healing to others just like he used the disciples. There are major miracles happening in other countries. I heard a minister say he believes the western world does not see miracles like other parts of the world because we have so many options. We seek the doctors first and other avenues, then the Lord when all else fells. Other countries have no options. Jesus is their only option, and He does not disappoint them. It's just like in the Old Testament; blind eyes are being opened, the deaf are hearing, the crippled are walking, and even people being raised from the dead. Now, I know that some of you just entertained the thought, *I don't know if I believe that.*

Well you don't have to, but healing will not work for you.

The Lord is using me in healing ministry, and I have seen many miracles take place. He will use anyone who is willing because you are a vessel in which He operates through, and if He chooses to work through you, it's not because you're special; it's that you made yourself available.

> Praise the Lord oh my soul, and forget not all his benefits – who forgives all your sins and heals all your disease.
>
> (Psalm 103:2-3)

> He sent his word, and healed them, and delivered them from their destructions.
>
> (Psalm 107:20)

This process of standing on God's Word for healing is exactly what Dodie Olsteen did when she was diagnosed with stage four lung cancer. She was sent home to die. That was over twenty years ago, and she is still alive today. God's Word is true. From this day forward I want all of you to confess everyday, "My youth is renewed like the eagles. God wants me healed, therefore, I am healed. Amen."

Power in Relationship

Many people have become so use to religious tradition and the laws of man that they forget about God's law. Jesus said that God's commandments are made of none effective by traditions of men(Matthew 15:6). This scripture is referring to religious customs, legends, intellectual practices, and man-made religious teachings.

> So then, just as you received Christ Jesus as Lord, continue to live your lives in Him, rooted and built up in Him, strengthened in the faith as you were taught, and overflowing with thankfulness. See to it that no one takes you captive through hollow and deceptive philosophy, which depends on human tradition and the elemental spiritual forces of this world rather than on Christ.
>
> (Colossians 2:6-8)

When thinking of God many see him as an historical figure, remembering the heartfelt scene of Jesus dying on the cross. I believe in many cases people believe the story ended there. Forgetting the fact that Jesus died for our sins, He bore all of our infirmities, went down to the depths of hell, took the keys from Satan, He rose again on the third day, and today sits at the right hand of the Father. He is not dead. Jesus is living and desperately wants to be a part of our lives today if we would allow Him.

> For as Jonas was three days and three nights in the whale's belly; so shall the Son of man be three days and three nights in the heart of the earth.
>
> (Matthew 12:40)

> I am the God of Abraham, and the God of Isaac, and the God of Jacob? God is not the God of the dead, but of the living.
>
> (Matthew 22:32)

Many Christians go to church every Sunday and worship and praise the Lord, then leave, never saying a prayer or even acknowledging God's existence the rest of the week. Many are living a life of heartache, brokenness, stress, depression, and every type of sickness and disease. What kind of example is that for the unsaved? Why would the unsaved want to be saved if that is the life of a Christian? God wants so much more for us than that.

God wants his people to be blessed in every area of life experiencing wholeness, and fullness, nothing missing, nothing broken; that is what the world needs to see in every believer's life.

> The Spirit of the Lord is upon me, because he hath anointed me to preach the gospel to the poor; he hath sent me to heal the brokenhearted, to preach deliverance to the captives, and recovering of sight to the blind, to set at liberty them that are bruised.
>
> (Luke 4:18)

> Verily, verily, I say unto you, He that believeth on me, the works that I do shall he do also; and greater works than these shall he do; because I go unto my Father.
>
> (John 14:12)

The Bible is a covenant to the believer. It is our manual to help us live a successful life here on this earth, not when we get to heaven. When you purchase a car or an appliance from the store you receive an owner's manual. So why would we expect any less? Is not a human being much more complicated and important than a car or an appliance? The Bible is the living word inspired by the Holy Ghost, and should be read every day. The scriptures state it is life to those who find it and health to all their flesh.

There is a religious system that includes all the religions in the world; even Christianity. Jesus never came to birth a religion, but He came to birth a family on the earth. He came to birth and produce His Bride, and there are many in the church that do not know God.

We must seek to have an intimate relationship with God the Son (Jesus) and God the Holy Spirit. In addition to reading the Word, praise and worship is an essential part of that relationship. Praise and worship are the ways to Father's heart.

> But the hour cometh, and now is, when the true worshippers shall worship the Father in spirit and in truth: for the Father seeketh such to worship Him.
>
> (John 4:23)

We can worship Him by spending time alone with him having an honest heartfelt conversation praising, thanking, and speaking of His goodness. Thank Him for bringing you out of past trials you were facing. Don't focus on what you don't have, but thank Him for what you do have. Thank Him for the fact that you realize your situation could be much worse if it weren't for his mercy and grace. Let Him know that you take nothing for granted and appreciate every favor and blessing. First, let me say you can praise and worship anywhere: in the car, or at work, and the focus is only on Him, not asking for anything. My best times of praise and worship take place in my bedroom. I begin my praise with singing songs. One of my favorite songs that sets the tone is "You Have Been So Good." Some of the lyrics are, "You have been so good to me, in my faithless hour you've been my strength." These words cause me to reflect over my life and recall how good God has been. He has brought me through some difficult times. During praise the thankfulness turns to worship. Worship is the act of adoration, love, honor, respect. I start worshipping Him for who He is, Holy Father (Names of God) my El Shaddai, Lord God Almighty, Jehovah-Raah, The Lord My Shepherd, Jehovah-Jireh, The Lord My Provider, or Adonai—Lord, Master. It is when you are in true worship that the Glory of the Lord appears.

Something happens inside when you enter into a pure worship; it is great. I not only feel an inner cleansing or peace take place, but I experience the tangible manifestation of His presence. The atmosphere in the room changes and I feel the weighty presence of God. When this happens you began to look forward to those times alone with Him. Once the Glory is manifested, you can leave the room and come back and the presence will still be there. When you worship the next day, it's easier to enter in.

In Hebrew it is called the *Kvod adonai*, which means the shekinah glory of the Lord. Kvod (Glory) in Hebrew means *weight*. In the Old Testament many saw God's shekinah glory as the physical manifestation of the presence of God.

By him therefore let us offer the sacrifice of praise to God continually, that is, the fruit of our lips giving thanks to his name.

(Hebrew 13:15)

You can fellowship with Him throughout the day. When you have a friend you can talk to them about anything. It is the same with the Lord; you can talk to him about things you would not feel comfortable talking about with anyone else. You remember the old hymn, "What a Friend We Have in Jesus?" These are not just clichés. If you feel that you don't currently have a relationship with Jesus start today. Talk to Him and say whatever you feel led to say. Just do it with a sincere heart.

Conclusion

I have shared with you principles and precepts from God's Word that I have put to work in my personal life. Any success I have enjoyed has been the result of a personal relationship with Jesus and a rich prayer life. Let me lead you into the throne room of God. You can enjoy the very best life He has to offer and experience the success God desires for you.

Prayer

Heavenly Father, I approach Your throne boldly in the Name of Jesus. I have seen from Your Word that You desire to be personally involved in my life. It is Your desire to answer my prayers. I believe that Jesus died and suffered the punishment for my sins so I could experience a close relationship with You as my heavenly Father.

I can see from Your Word that I have the right to expect my prayers to be answered, not based on my worthiness, but based on my right standing in Christ Jesus. Your Word says if I draw near to You, You will draw near to me. I desire a more personal relationship with You and want to experience a rich and successful prayer life. I thank You for the love You have expressed toward me through Your Word. I will respond to that love right now and expect You to manifest Yourself in my life as I act on Your Word of faith. As I apply the principles I have learned, I expect to see the results. I thank you and praise you for your faithfulness, in Jesus Name. Amen!

Prayer for Salvation and Baptism in the Holy Spirit

Heavenly Father I come to you in the name of Jesus. Your word says, that whosoever shall call on the name of the Lord shall be saved (Acts 2:21). I am calling on you. I pray and ask Jesus to come into my heart and be Lord over my life, according to Romans 10:9-10: "If thou shalt confess with thy mouth the Lord Jesus, and shalt believe in thine heart that God hath raised him from the dead. Thou shalt be saved. For with the heart man believeth unto righteousness; and with the mouth confession is made unto salvation." I do that now. I confess that Jesus is Lord, and I believe in my heart that God raised him from the dead. I am now reborn!

I am a Christian, a child of Almighty God. Father you also said in your Word, "If ye then, being evil, know how to give good gifts unto your children; How much more shall your heavenly Father give the Holy Spirit to them that ask him?" (Luke 11:13). I am also asking you to fill me with the Holy Spirit. Holy Spirit rise up in me as I praise God. I fully expect to speak with other tongues as you give me utterance (Acts 2:4). In Jesus name. Amen!

Begin to praise God for filling you with the Holy Spirit. Speak those words and syllables you receive, not in your own language, but the language given to you by the Holy Spirit. You have to use your own voice. God will not force you to speak. And don't be concerned with how it sounds. It is a heavenly language! Now find a good church that boldly preaches God's word and obeys it. Become a part of that church. We need to be connected together; it increases our strength in God. It is God's plan for us.